Guitar Book with
Online Video & Audio Access

Taught By
Jody Worrell

To access Online Audio & Video for this course, go to the following web address:

http://cvls.com/extras/srv/

The Author

Jody Worrell has been a professional performer and teacher in the Atlanta area for over 30 years. He has recorded and appeared on stage domestically and internationally with such artists as Lyle Lovett, Mitch Ryder and the Detroit Wheels, Badfinger, Delbert McClinton, Phil Collins, The Marvelettes, The Drifters, The Tokens, The Crystals, Derek Trucks, and many others. Jody plays all styles on demand, but always returns to the blues, taking an approach which is based in tradition, but always seeking to expand harmonic boundaries. He also has to his credit four of the many Watch & Learn products: *Let's Jam! CD Blues & Rock Vol. 3*, *Let's Jam! CD Country Vol. 2*, *Let's Jam! Blues Standards*, and *Blues Licks & Solos*.

Jody studied classical guitar briefly with the legendary John Sutherland, but attributes his playing mostly to hard work, open-mindedness to diverse types of music, and to the indelible mark left by long-time teacher, mentor and friend, Merrill Dilbeck.

Jody has produced almost three hundred video lessons on blues, rock, and country for GuitarCompass.com.

How To Use The Book & Video

Step 1 - Watch the Video while following along with the book. Play along with the Video on your guitar. Replay each chapter on the Video until you are comfortable playing along with it.

Step 2 - When you are comfortable with a lesson or piece of music, try playing along with the audio track for each lesson on the Video. You'll find these on the Chapter Menus. Try expanding your horizons a little and stretch out your technique. Don't be afraid to experiment.

Step 3 - Go back to the book & Video and play along to make sure you're on the right track.

TABLE OF CONTENTS

About This Course

Stevie Ray Vaughan Style is the first installment in the *In The Style Of The Legends Series*. All courses include two full length DVDs packed full of famous licks and solos as interpreted by Jody Worrell. The courses are in the style of legendary guitarists such as Stevie Ray Vaughan, Eric Clapton, Jimi Hendrix, B.B. King, David Gilmour, and more.

Each lick and solo is broken down and the techniques and timing of each phrase is totally explained and played several times. Close-ups and split screens are used to make learning even clearer. In addition to the video instruction, there are full band practice tracks allowing the students to practice with a professional band anytime they want to perfect their timing and technique.

A book is included with the two DVDs that has standard music notation and tablature for everything that is taught. The type face is large for ease of viewing.

The *In The Style Of The Legends DVD Series* is based on content developed during 15 years of producing lessons for GuitarCompass.com which have been viewed by millions of guitarists. If you like these DVDs and want more high quality lessons, go to GuitarCompass.com to see our Free Lessons and Premium Lessons.

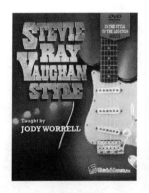 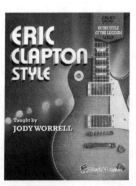 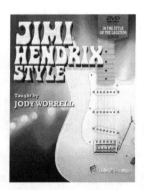  

To access Online Audio & Video for this course, go to the following web address:

http://cvls.com/extras/srv/

TUNING, TABLATURE,
& TECHNIQUES

TUNING THE GUITAR

Before playing the guitar, it must be tuned to standard pitch. If you have a piano at home, it can be used as a tuning source. The following picture shows which note on the piano to tune each open string of the guitar to.

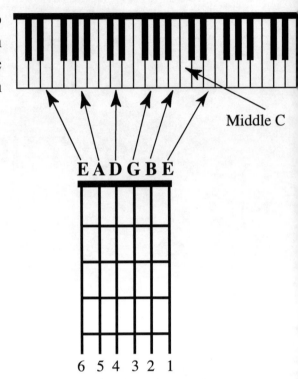

Electronic Tuner

An electronic tuner is the fastest and most accurate way to tune a guitar. We highly recommend getting one. They are available for $15 and up.

Note: Stevie Ray commonly tuned 1/2 step below standard tuning. These lessons are presented in standard tuning so you won't have to retune your guitar.

TABLATURE

This book is written in both tablature and standard music notation. We will explain tablature because it is easy to learn if you are teaching yourself and because a lot of popular guitar music is available in tablature.

Tablature is a system for writing music that shows the proper string and fret to play. In guitar tablature, each line represents a string on the guitar. If the string is to be fretted, the fret number is written on the appropriate line. Otherwise a 0 is written. Study the examples below until you understand them thoroughly.

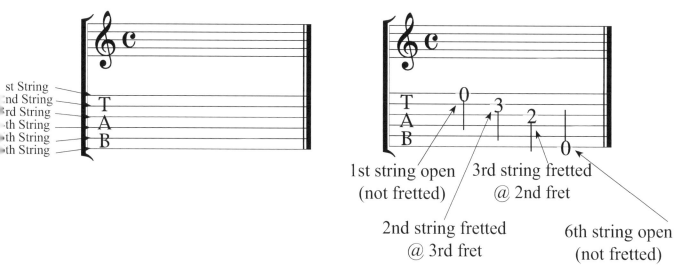

The music will be divided into two sets of lines (staffs).

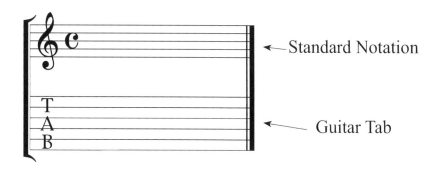

TECHNIQUES

Here are some fundamental techniques that are used this course.

Hammer-ons & Pull-offs

When playing a hammer-on, pick the first note, then hammer-on with a finger on your left hand. You will need to be on the tip of the finger and strike the note with velocity and accuracy.

When playing a pull-off, again pick the first note, then pull-off with a finger on your left hand. Once again, use the tip of the finger. The finger you are pulling off to needs to hold the string stable during the pull off.

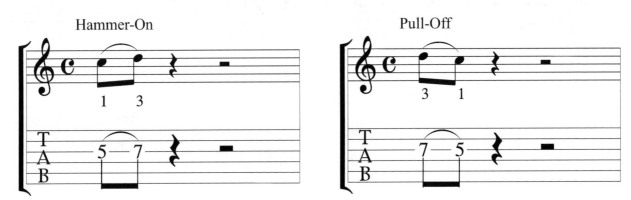

Double Hammer-ons & Pull-offs

A double hammer-on is executed by picking the first note and hammering on the next two notes. When pulling off, you should feel as if you're plucking the string with your finger. Both techniques require you to be on the tip of your fingers.

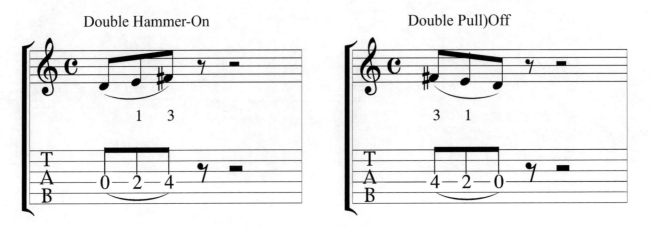

Hammer-on & Pull-off Combination

This technique starts by picking the first note, hammering on, and then pulling off back to the first note.

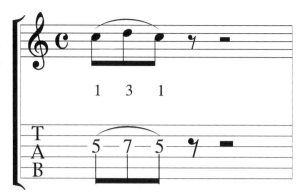

Slides

A slide means you pick a note and slide into another. Slides can move up or down and can be phrased many different ways.

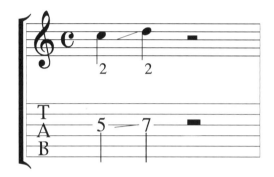
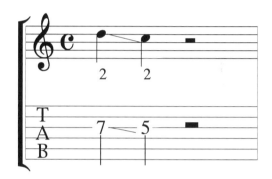

Slides From An Undetermined Note

This slide usually starts a fret or two away but sometimes further. It does not stay at the starting point long enough for the listener to really tell where it starts.

Double Stop Slides

This is a slide involving two notes. It is important that both fingers move evenly across the frets.

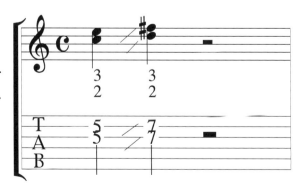

Bends

When playing a bend, use all the fingers that are available to help execute the bend. For example, use the third finger to bend the note, the second finger on the same string helping to bend the note, and the first finger to mute the string above it.

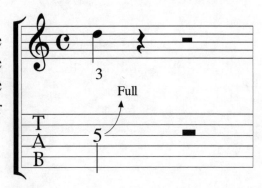

Double Stop Bends

Use your pinky to hold the note stationary on the first string and use the third and second finger to bend the second string a whole step. You can play them both at the same time or one after the other.

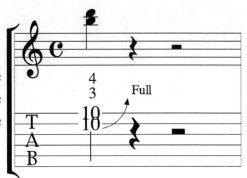

Hammer-On With A Bend

This is a very legato sound. Hammer-on to the seventh fret and then bend the note a whole step. You only pick the first note.

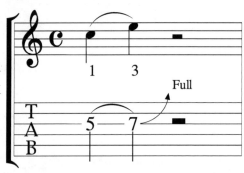

STEVIE RAY VAUGHAN

STYLE

LICKS IN A

The Licks In A lessons use Track 11, *Bump In The Road*, from *Let's Jam! CD Blues & Rock Vol 3*.

Licks In A Part 1

We'll learn five licks in the style of Stevie Ray Vaughan. We'll capture a few of his trademark bends and slurs and discuss his approach to tone as well. The Video will cover some of the music theory behind each lick as well as give you an opportunity to "trade" the licks back and forth in a jam situation. All of these licks are in the key of A and will focus on the A7 chord.

Lick 1

Lick 1 starts with a four note pickup or lead in. Check the Video for the exact timing.

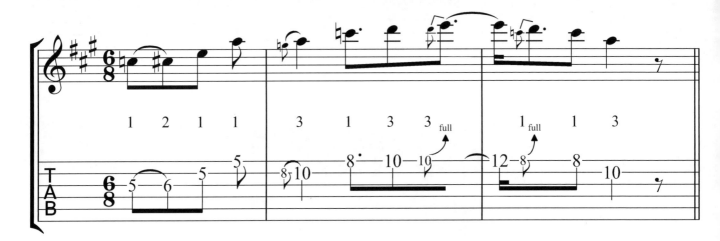

Demo

Each phrase will be played along with a backing track at the correct speed.

Trading Licks

Each lick will be traded back & forth. I'll play it first, then leave space for you to play it right after so you can compare your tone, timing, and articulation. Take your time and work on this section until you can play it perfectly all three times through.

Video & Audio Access

To access Audio & Video for this course, go to this web address:
http://cvls.com/extras/srv/

8

Lick 2

We'll use the same format for each lick. Each lick will be taught in detail. Next it will be played at full speed along with a backing track. Then it will be traded back and forth, leaving space for you to play right after me.

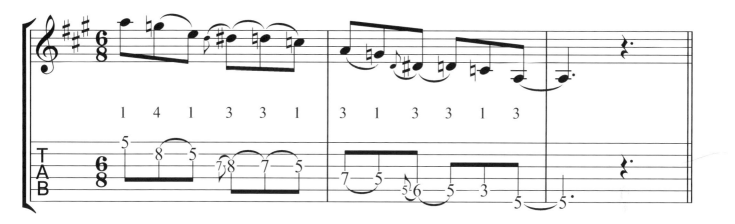

Lick 3

Lick 3 starts with a three note pickup or lead in. This is a classic Stevie sounding lick with a lot of double stops and notes ringing through.

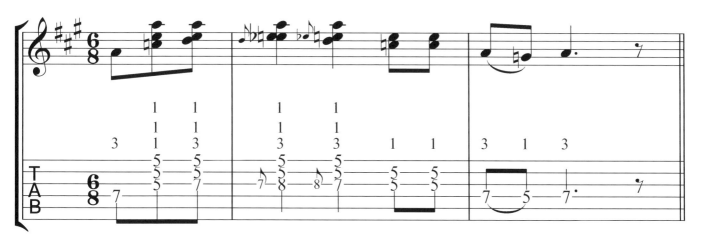

Note: You'll get the most from these lessons by taking your time and practicing each lick until you've mastered it. That's when you'll really be able to retain the licks and bring them into your day to day playing.

Lick 4

Listen to the Video to get the classic Stevie unbending sound in the second bar.

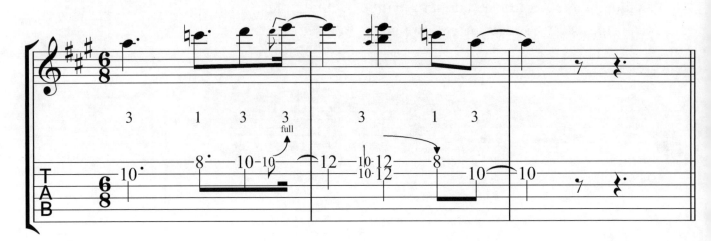

Lick 5

This lick starts with a bend and release. Listen to the Video for details.

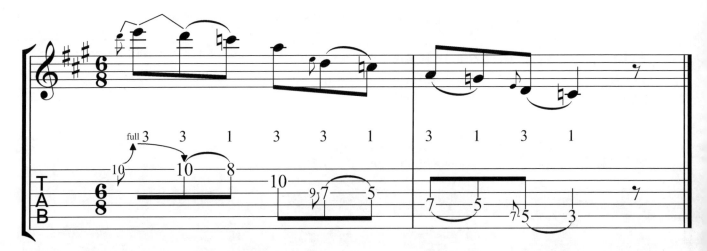

Playing With Jam Track

Now we'll play all five licks along with the audio track in a random order. When you get to the point where you can pick and choose them as you like, you're well on your way to owning the licks and you can use them in your day to day playing.

To access Audio & Video for this course, go to this web address:
http://cvls.com/extras/srv/

10

Licks In A Part 2

This lesson will look at another series of guitar licks inspired by Stevie Ray Vaughan that focus on his trademark bends and slurs as well as his approach to tone. We'll cover each lick in detail by examining the techniques required to play the lick and the music theory behind it.

Lick 1

This lick uses Stevie's unique approach to using chords shapes along with bends to achieve that signature sound.

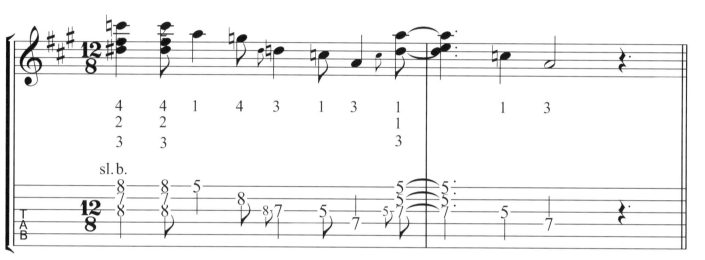

Demo

Each phrase will be played along with a backing track at the correct speed.

Trading Licks

Each lick will be traded back & forth. I'll play it first, then leave space for you to play it right after so you can compare your tone, timing, and articulation. Take your time and work on this section until you can play it perfectly all three times through.

Video & Audio Access

To access Audio & Video for this course, go to this web address:
http://cvls.com/extras/srv/

11

Lick 2

This lick uses a lot of slides both upward and downward. We're using the fourth finger a lot, but you can substitute the ring finger if you're not comfortable using the fourth.

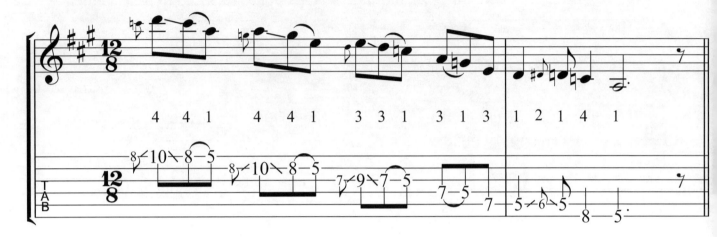

Lick 3

This lick uses the familiar sound of striking adjacent strings along with the bent note. Listen to the Video for details.

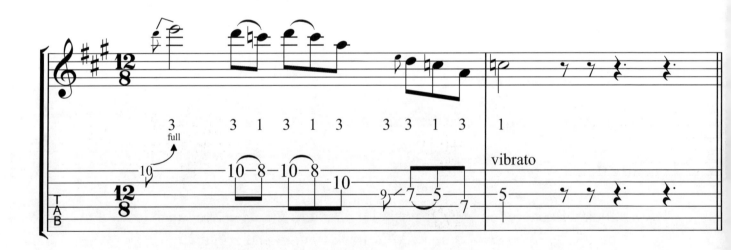

Note: Another great drill is to play the licks with me as well as in between in the trading section. Try this for all five licks in this section.

Lick 4

This lick uses big bends, double stops, and double slides.

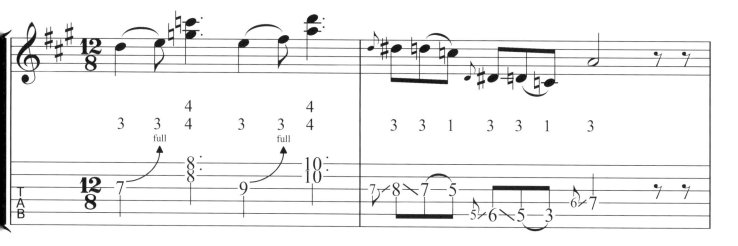

Lick 5

Here's a crazy little lick moving up the neck using double stops and slides.

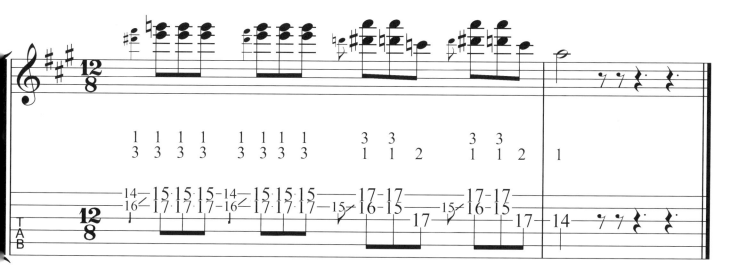

Playing With The Jam Track

Now we'll play all five licks along with the audio track in a random order. When you get to the point where you can pick and choose them as you like, you're well on your way to owning the licks and you can use them in your day to day playing.

To access Audio & Video for this course, go to this web address:
http://cvls.com/extras/srv/

STEVIE RAY VAUGHAN STYLE SWING SOLOS

The Swing Solo lessons use Track 11, *In The Swing In Bb*, from *Let's Jam! CD Blues & Rock Vol 3*.

Swing Solo 1

This lesson will teach you a 12 bar blues guitar solo in Bb and draws on Stevie Ray Vaughan's inspired lead playing over a groove with a Texas Swing. I will teach you how to play each section of the solo while highlighting the techniques that gave Stevie Ray his unique sound. This solo is played over the *In The Swing In Bb* audio track from *Let's Jam! CD Blues & Rock Volume 3*. We will start by playing the complete solo along with the jam track and then break the solo into three phrases.

Phrase 1

The first phrase starts with a three note pickup or lead in and uses half step slides.

Demo

Each phrase will be played along with a backing track at the correct speed.

Trading Licks

Each lick will be traded back & forth. I'll play it first, then leave space for you to play it right after so you can compare your tone, timing, and articulation. Take your time and work on this section until you can play it perfectly all three times through.

Video & Audio Access

To access Audio & Video for this course, go to this web address:
http://cvls.com/extras/srv/

15

Phrase 2

Start with notes from the Eb7 chord

Phrase 3

Phrase 3 starts with the last two notes from Phrase 2 as a pickup or lead in.

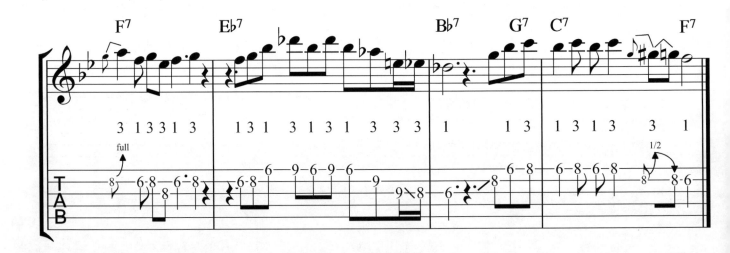

Playing With The Jam Track

Play the complete solo along with the jam track. You can access the file from the following web address:

http://cvls.com/extras/srv/

Stevie Ray Swing Style Solo 1

By Jody Worrell

Phrase #1

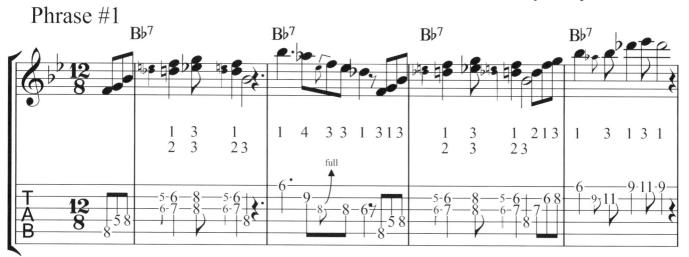

Phrase #2

Phrase #3

Swing Solo 2

This is a follow up to Swing Solo 1, again playing over a Texas Swing blues groove. In addition to teaching a great blues solo, I will provide detailed instruction on specific techniques that Stevie Ray used to create his signature style.

Phrase 1

Once again, start with a pickup or lead in phrase. We'll use a series of bends and releases in bar 3.

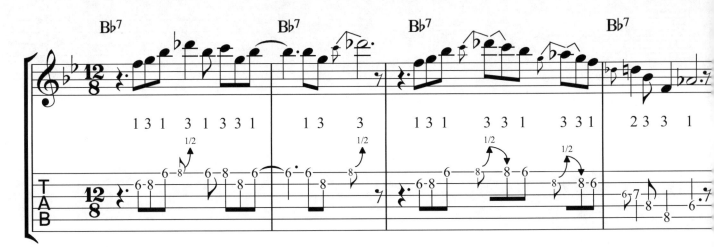

Demo

Each phrase will be played along with a backing track at the correct speed.

Trading Licks

Each lick will be traded back & forth. I'll play it first, then leave space for you to play it right after so you can compare your tone, timing, and articulation. Take your time and work on this section until you can play it perfectly all three times through.

Video & Audio Access

To access Audio & Video for this course, go to this web address:
http://cvls.com/extras/srv/

18

Phrase 2

Phrase 2 starts with the classic Stevie move of a whole step bend on the 3rd string followed by the 6th fret on the 2nd and 1st strings. Listen to the Video for details.

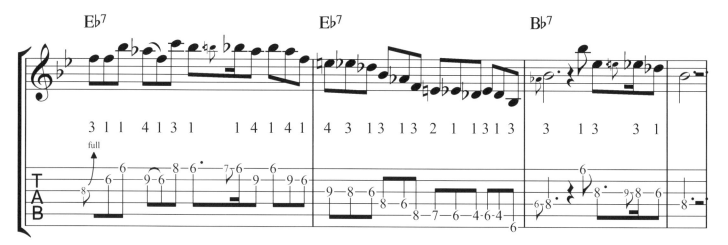

Phrase 3

Start with a series of double stops. These can be played with or without slides. Listen to the Video for details.

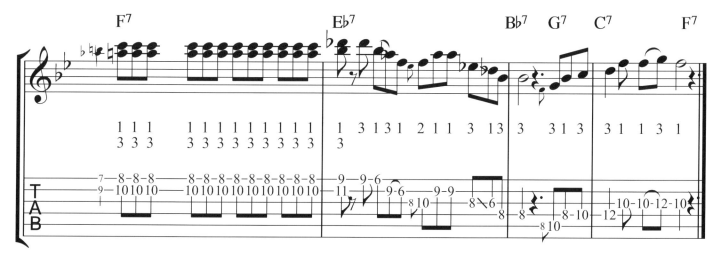

Playing With The Jam Track

Play the complete solo along with the jam track. You can access the file from the following web address:

http://cvls.com/extras/srv/

Stevie Ray Swing Style Solo 2

Phrase #1

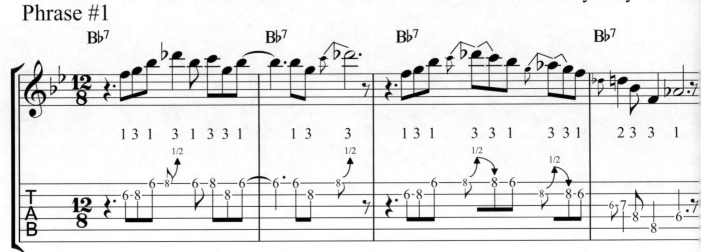

Phrase #2

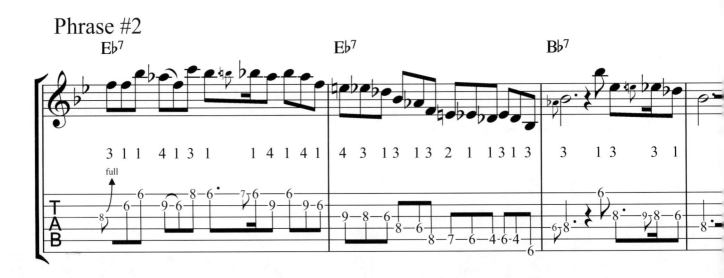

Phrase #3

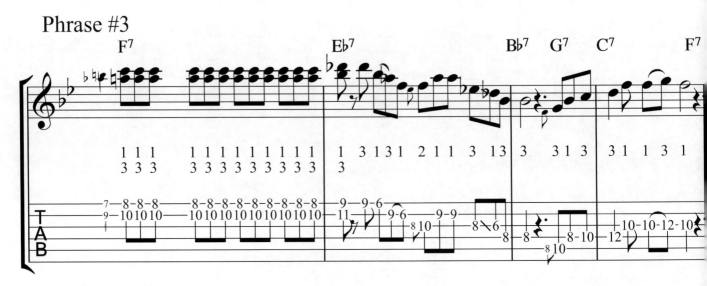

STEVIE RAY VAUGHAN
STYLE
MINOR SOLOS

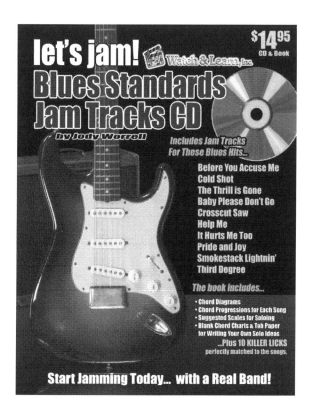

The Minor Solo lessons use Track 7, *Help Me,* from *Let's Jam! Blues Standards* book and CD.

Minor Solo 1

This lesson will teach you a blues guitar solo in the style of guitar legend Stevie Ray Vaughan. This solo is played over a three chord A minor blues progression and features licks out of the minor pentatonic and minor blues scales. I will walk you through playing this solo in detail paying special attention to the vibrato and bending that gave Stevie his signature sound.

Phrase 1

Listen to the Video to learn how to mute the sound after bending notes by using your pick.

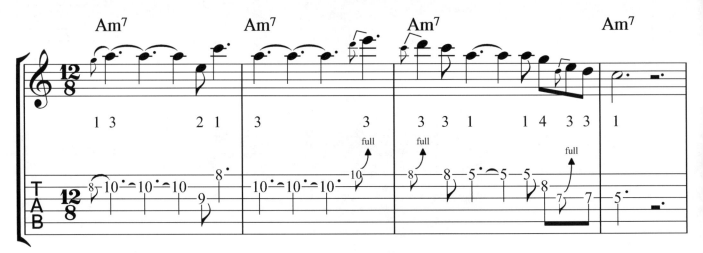

Demo

Each phrase will be played along with a backing track at the correct speed.

Trading Licks

Each lick will be traded back & forth. I'll play it first, then leave space for you to play it right after so you can compare your tone, timing, and articulation. Take your time and work on this section until you can play it perfectly all three times through.

Video & Audio Access

To access Audio & Video for this course, go to this web address:
http://cvls.com/extras/srv/

Phrase 2

Phrase 2 starts with the classic blues lick that we used in *Swing Solo 2*, but in a different position on the guitar neck.

Phrase 3

Phrase 3 starts with slides in the Em position and also uses the classic blues lick from Phrase 2 in a different position.

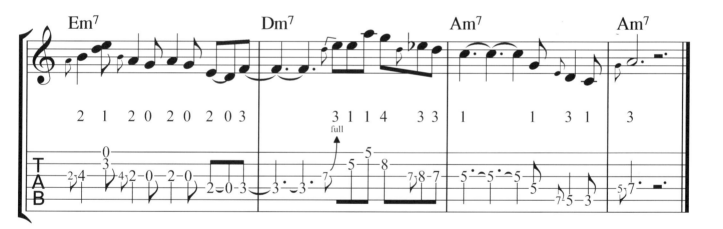

Playing With The Jam Track

Play the complete solo along with the jam track. You can access the file from the following web address:

http://cvls.com/extras/srv/

Stevie Ray Style Minor Solo 1

By Jody Worrell

Phrase 1

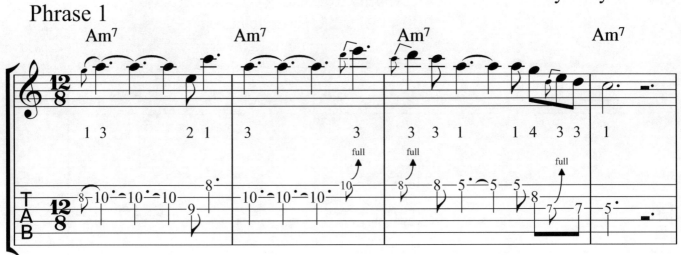

Phrase 2

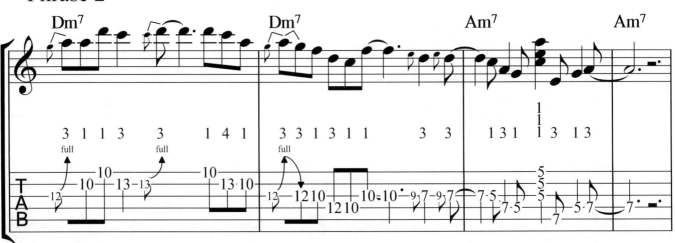

Phrase 3

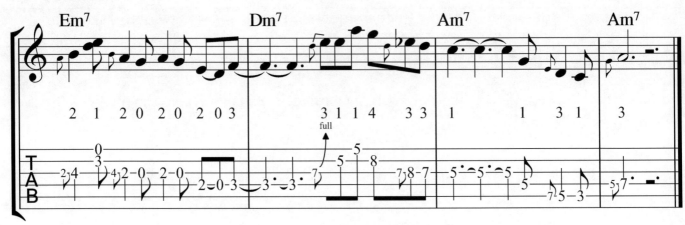

Minor Solo 2

This lesson will build on *Minor Solo 1* by teaching you a harder and more advanced solo in A minor. This solo features lots of Stevie-style bending, slurs, hammer-ons, and pull-offs. I will break the solo down for you into four bar sections. You will learn how to play the solo note by note and get to practice with jam tracks that loop each section.

Phrase 1

Phrase 1 uses several techniques we learned earlier in this course.

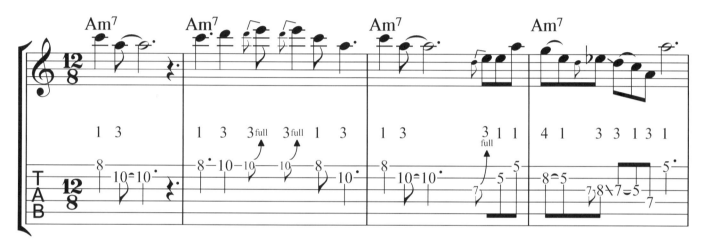

Demo

Each phrase will be played along with a backing track at the correct speed.

Trading Licks

Each lick will be traded back & forth. I'll play it first, then leave space for you to play it right after so you can compare your tone, timing, and articulation. Take your time and work on this section until you can play it perfectly all three times through.

Video & Audio Access

To access Audio & Video for this course, go to this web address:
http://cvls.com/extras/srv/

Phrase 2

This phrase starts by using sixths with slides. Listen to the Video for details.

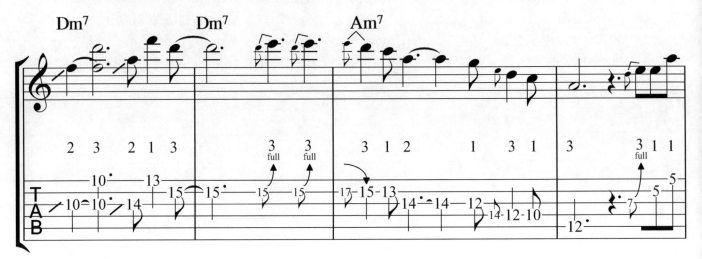

Phrase 3

Start with the last three notes from Phrase 2, the classic blues lick again.

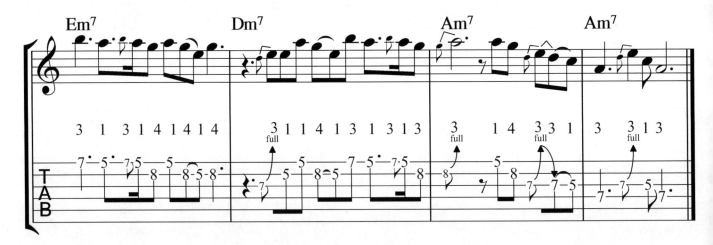

Playing With The Jam Track

Play the complete solo along with the jam track. You can access the file from the following web address:

http://cvls.com/extras/srv/

Stevie Ray Style Minor Solo 2

By Jody Worrell

Phrase #1

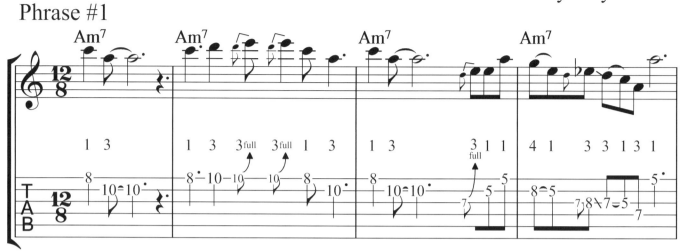

Phrase #2

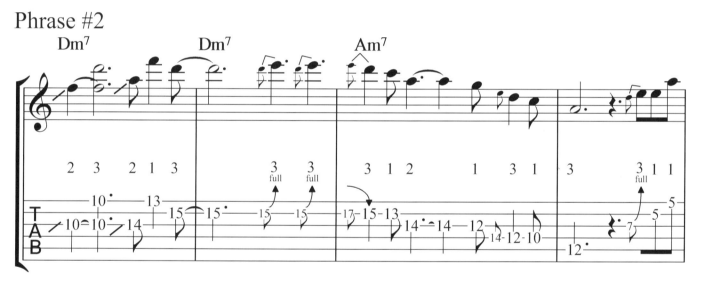

Phrase #3

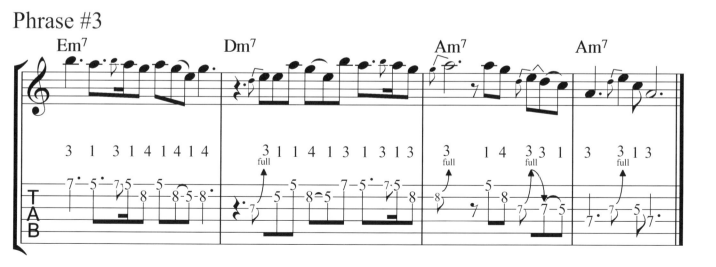

27

Made in United States
Troutdale, OR
07/06/2024